COSTUME, TRADITION, AND CULTURE:
REFLECTING ON THE PAST

Roman Myths, Heroes, and Legends

by

Dwayne E. Pickels

Chelsea House Publishers
Philadelphia

CHELSEA HOUSE PUBLISHERS

Editor-in-Chief Stephen Reginald
Managing Editor James D. Gallagher
Production Manager Pamela Loos
Art Director Sara Davis
Picture Editor Judy Hasday
Senior Production Editor Lisa Chippendale
Designer Takeshi Takahashi

3 5 7 9 8 6 4 2

Library of Congress Cataloging-in-Publication Data

Pickels, Dwayne E.
Roman myths, heroes, and legends / by Dwayne E. Pickels.

   p. cm. — (Costume, tradition, and culture: reflecting on the past)
Includes bibliographical references and index.
Summary: Presents biographical sketches of twenty–five gods and goddesses of Roman mythology, from Apollo to Vesta.

ISBN 0–7910–5164–1 (hardcover)
1. Mythology, Roman—Juvenile literature. [1. Mythology, Roman.] I. Title. II. Series.
BL802.P494 1998   98–29113
398.2'0937'01—dc21   CIP
                                              AC

CONTENTS

INTRODUCTION

For as long as people have known that other cultures existed, they have been curious about the differences in their customs and traditions. Julius Caesar, the famous Roman leader, wrote long chronicles about the inhabitants of Gaul (modern-day France) while he was leading troops in the Gallic Wars (58–51 B.C.). In the chronicles, he discussed their religious beliefs, their customs, their day-to-day life, and the conflicts among the different groups. Explorers like Marco Polo traveled thousands of miles and devoted years of their lives to learning about the peoples of the East and bringing home the stories of Chinese court life, along with the silks, spices, and inventions of that culture. The Chelsea House series *Costume, Tradition, and Culture: Reflecting on the Past* continues this legacy of exploration and discovery by discussing some of the most fascinating traditions, beliefs, legends, and artifacts from around the world.

Different cultures develop traditions and costumes to mark the roles of people in their societies, to commemorate events in their histories, and to make the changes and mysteries of life more meaningful. Soldiers wear uniforms to show that they are serving in their nation's army, and insignia on the uniforms show what ranks they hold within the army. People of Bukhara, a city in Uzbekistan, have for centuries woven fine threads of gold into their clothes, and when they travel to other cities they can be recognized as Bukharans by the golden embroidery on their traditional costume. For many years, in the Irish countryside, people would leave bowls of milk outside at night as an offering to the fairies, or "Good People," believing that this would help ensure their favor and keep the family safe from fairy mischief. In Mexico, November 2 is the Day of the Dead, when people visit cemeteries and have feasts to remember their ancestors. In the United States, brides wear white dresses, and the traditional wedding includes many rituals: the father of the bride "giving her away" to the groom, the exchange of vows and rings, the throwing of rice, the tossing of the bride's bouquet. These rituals and symbols help make the marriage meaningful and special for the couple, their families, and their friends, by expressing the change that is taking place and allowing the friends and families to wish luck to the couple.

This series will explore some of the myths, symbols, costumes, and traditions of various cultures from around the world and different times in the past. *Fighting Units of the American War of Independence,* for example, will detail the uniforms, weapons, and decorations of the regiments and battalions on both sides of the war, along with the battles in which they became famous. *Roman Myths, Heroes, and Legends* describes how the ancient Romans explained the wonders and natural phenomena of their world with fantastic stories of superhuman heroes and almost human deities who could change the course of history at will. In *Popular Superstitions,* you will learn how some familiar superstitious beliefs—such as throwing spilled salt over your shoulder, or hanging a horseshoe over your door for good luck—originally began, in times when people feared that devils and evil spirits were meddling in their lives. Few people still believe in malicious spirits, but many still toss the spilled salt over their shoulders, or knock on wood when expressing cautious hope. The legendary figures of a culture—the brave explorers of *The Wild West* or the wicked brigands described in *Infamous Pirates*—help shape that culture's values by providing grand, almost mythical examples of what people should (or should not!) strive to be.

The illustrations that accompany these books have their own cultural history. Originally, they were printed on small collectors' cards and sold in the early 20th century. Each card in a set of 25 or 50 would depict a different person, artifact, or event, and usually the reverse side would offer a few sentences of description to explain the picture. Now, they provide a fascinating glimpse into history and an entertaining addition to the stories presented here.

ABOUT THE AUTHOR

DWAYNE E. PICKELS is an award-winning reporter with the *Greensburg (Pa.) Tribune-Review*. A magna cum laude graduate of the University of Pittsburgh, where he cofounded and edited the literary magazine *Pendulum,* Dwayne won a Pennsylvania Newspaper Publishers' Association (PNPA) Keystone Press Award in 1992. The author of a number of books for Chelsea House, Dwayne lives in Scottdale, Pennsylvania, with his wife, Mary, and their daughter, Kaidia Leigh. In his free time, he is currently immersed in a number of literary pursuits—which include a novel based on Celtic myth and legend. In addition to writing, Dwayne enjoys outdoor excursions, including bird watching, hiking, photography, and target shooting . . . along with typically futile attempts at fishing.

OVERVIEW

Roman Myths

T he classical wonder that came to be known as the Roman Empire was built in part on the conquest of many smaller kingdoms. Those conquered cultures had numerous religious systems, traditional stories, and legends. But of all the peoples absorbed into the Roman Empire, it was the Greeks whose religion and legends played the largest role.

The gods of Roman mythology were primarily adapted from Greek gods and given new names. The Greek Cronus became the Roman Saturn, Zeus became Jupiter, and so on. Not only were these marvelous casts of gods assimilated into the Roman religion, but so were, in many cases, their grand, heroic, and sometimes racy story lines. Today, embellished by poets and historians through the ages, their names, traits, and escapades have worked their way into our own culture. They are evident in our language itself—most obviously in the words we use to identify days of the week, months of the year, and objects in the heavens. We even use the names of Roman gods for some of our modern technological marvels—for instance, we have given the name Saturn to a rocket and Apollo to a space program.

For those reasons we should strive to know a little something about the peculiar beings the Romans labeled gods. Besides, the Roman deities, along with the other great heroes of Roman legend, are in many ways just exaggerated mirrors of ourselves. They help us see what we might be like if we were elevated to a higher plane of existence than normal humans can reach in today's day-to-day world. And that is no shabby feat for a group of beings who never existed.

Or did they exist? Maybe the greatest power of myth is its ability to challenge our cultures and beliefs—things we may simply have accepted as fact over the course of our lives. Perhaps, at least, we can learn more about who and what we are—where we came from and where we are going—by thinking about the gods and heroes of the ancient Romans.

APOLLO

Though there were several gods with the name Apollo, the one most revered was the son of Jupiter and Latona. Apollo was considered by many to be the god of fine arts, medicine, music, poetry, and eloquence, and also the god of prophecy and archery. In later years, and especially in the Roman pantheon, he was the sun god.

Apollo and his twin sister, the goddess Diana, were born on the island of Delos. According to some variations of the legend, Neptune set up the island as a safe place to protect Latona from Jupiter's jealous wife, Juno.

Apollo later joined Juno and Neptune in a revolt against his father, Jupiter. This occurred after Jupiter's immoral escapades went beyond what the gods could bear. The unsuccessful rebellion earned Apollo and Neptune a temporary stint as unwilling servants.

During more peaceful times, Apollo was a gifted musician who delighted the gods with the music of his lyre (an ancient kind of harp). He was also a master archer and a strong, fast, and agile athlete.

Apollo took many lovers, though he never married. He pursued a mountain nymph named Daphne, but she was rescued by Gaia (Mother Earth), who turned her into a laurel tree. Ever after, the laurel was Apollo's favorite tree.

At another time, Apollo had his eye on the goddess of the dawn, Aurora. But he learned she had been wooed by the giant Orion, who spent much of his time hunting with Apollo's sister Diana. Jealous, Apollo managed to trick Diana into killing Orion. In her grief over her friend's demise, Diana put Orion's likeness among the stars, creating the constellation that we call Orion.

AURORA

Aurora, the goddess of the dawn, is often represented driving a rose-colored chariot drawn by white horses. In other illustrations she opens the gates of the east, and her rosy fingers pour dew on the earth.

Called Eos by the Greeks, Aurora heralded the daily journey of her brother, Helios, who drove the chariot that carried the sun. Each morning, after being aroused from slumber by the crowing of the rooster, she would rise to announce the start of her brother's journey. This was how people of the classical ages explained the earth's cycles of night and day. The announcing of the end of Helios's ride—in the west, at dusk—was the job of Aurora's sister Hespera. Their other sister was Selene, a goddess of the moon.

Aurora was married to Astraeus, and their children were the winds and the stars of the heavens. However, the less-than-faithful goddess also had many other lovers, even before she had a curse put on her by Venus, who caught her in the act with one of them—Venus's own lover, Mars. The curse was that Aurora would have an insatiable yearning for mortal companions—meaning that she would leave the male gods alone.

Among Aurora's many illegitimate children was Phaëton, who became notorious for his clumsy driving of the chariot of the sun. Phaëton lost control of the sun chariot and crashed, burning much of the earth. It seems Helios was the only one who could control the chariot. If Phaëton wasn't killed in the crash, he was slain by Jupiter as punishment for his foolishness.

BACCHUS

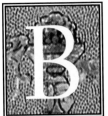

acchus, the god of wine, was the son of Jupiter and the nymph Semele. He is sometimes represented as a venerable old man with a beard, sometimes as a young man with horns, red face, and bloated body. Generally, though, he is seen as beautiful and rather effeminate.

His followers were primarily women. When under the influence of the wine god, these women would dance brazenly in the wilderness and set on the creatures of the forest with a savage frenzy, tearing the animals to pieces and feasting on their raw flesh and blood. Bacchus's name means "to revel," though the word is now more associated with fun and festivity than with the fierce reveling of some of his pagan followers.

Bacchus's birth was a strange event. When Juno, Jupiter's wife, found out that her husband had made Semele pregnant, she tricked the nymph into invoking Jupiter's wrath, and he struck her dead with one of his famous lightning bolts. Then one of the gods—some legends say it was Jupiter himself, others claim it was Mercury—rescued the unborn Bacchus from his dead mother's body and sewed him into Jupiter's thigh until he was old enough to be born. To spare the illegitimate child from Juno's further persecution, he was raised as a girl and even changed into a ram. In spite of these attempts to hide him from the jealous goddess, she made his life difficult until she finally drove him mad.

Often accompanied by satyrs (goat-men) and centaurs (horse-men), Bacchus taught mortals the arts of cultivating vineyards, making wine, and preparing honey. The Greeks knew Bacchus as Dionysus.

CERES

 ost commonly known as the goddess of the harvest and agriculture, Ceres was a daughter of Saturn and Ops. She was also one of the gods who were devoured by Saturn at birth and then set free by Jupiter. Her sisters were Juno and Vesta.

Though she never married, Ceres was beloved by both Jupiter and Neptune. Thus she became entangled in a dangerous web of emotion when she had several children by Jupiter. To escape the wrath of Neptune, Ceres fled and hid in a cavern unknown to any of the gods.

One of her children by Jupiter was Proserpine (or Persephone). The story of Proserpine represents the harvest goddess in her most famous role—that of the grieving mother. When Proserpine disappeared one day, Ceres searched the world far and wide to learn her daughter's fate. Eventually she was informed that the girl had been abducted by Pluto—dragged kicking and screaming through a crack in the earth into the Underworld, Pluto's dark realm. Ceres went to Jupiter and implored him to make the king of the Underworld hand over her daughter. Jupiter instead struck a deal: the girl could return to her mother for nine months of every year, but for the other three months she would stay with Pluto as his wife and queen of the Underworld.

This was how the ancients explained winter. It was the time that Proserpine spent in the Underworld. The remaining three-quarters of the year were the milder seasons of spring, summer, and fall.

Historically Ceres was worshiped under many different names, including Demeter. The word *cereal* derives from her Roman name.

CUPID

upid, known to the Greeks as Eros, was the Roman god of love. He was generally represented as a beautiful winged boy with a bow and arrows. He would shoot his arrows into the hearts of gods and mortals alike to make them fall in love. He also used torches on occasion to set lovers' hearts ablaze.

One of the most famous legends about Cupid concerns his love for the nymph Psyche. Cupid's mother, Venus, became jealous of Psyche's beauty, and she sent Cupid to punish the nymph. Instead, Cupid and Psyche fell in love, and he tried to ward off trouble by keeping his identity secret from her. If she looked on him, he warned Psyche, she would lose him forever.

But thanks to the villainous efforts of Psyche's two jealous sisters, she did look on him, and that caused him to tell his mother what had happened. Venus then imprisoned her son and launched a campaign of terror against the beautiful nymph. In spite of all that, the two lovers managed to get together in the end. Cupid escaped, saved Psyche from a deathlike sleep, and beseeched Jupiter to put an end to Venus's interference. Jupiter turned Psyche into an immortal by giving her nectar. He also blessed Cupid's union with her and ordered Venus to abide by his decision.

Today Cupid plays a large part in the observance of St. Valentine's Day.

DIANA

iana, twin sister of the god Apollo and daughter of Jupiter and Latona, was the goddess of the moon. She was known as a protector of springs and streams and as the guardian of wild animals and the woods. Also a goddess of chastity, she was revered by women and called on to ease them through childbirth. Most of all, however, she was known as a hunter.

One young man made the mistake of watching this chaste goddess bathe. For punishment, the goddess of the hunt turned him into a stag, and he was torn to death by his own hunting dogs.

It was through her love of the hunt that Diana met Orion, who was also a masterful hunter. The two became good friends, until her brother, Apollo, became jealous of Orion for winning the affections of Aurora, the goddess of the dawn. Apollo then tricked Diana into slaying Orion.

The Egyptians knew Diana as Isis. The Greeks called her Artemis. The Romans worshiped her as a celestial goddess under the name Luna, as a terrestrial goddess under the name Diana, and in the infernal regions as the deity Hecate.

In more modern times, under various names, Diana has been associated with some neo-pagan religions, such as the Wiccan faith.

ECHO

cho, a daughter of Ops, was a nymph whose gift of gab, so to speak, was much sought after by Jupiter. The ruler of the gods would persuade Echo to keep his wife, Juno, busy with gossip while he frolicked with other women.

When Juno finally saw through Jupiter's ruse and Echo's role in it, she exacted a punishment on Echo that some say befits the crime. She bound Echo's tongue, depriving her of the power of speech.

This predicament set the stage for the tragic second act of Echo's story. It seems that Juno's curse left Echo with only the ability to repeat the last few words that others said to her—thus the modern meaning of the word *echo*. In this state, Echo fell in love with Narcissus, a young man whose beauty caused all who looked on him to fall madly in love with him. The capacity to inspire devotion in so many people left him with a high opinion of himself, which eventually led to his downfall when the goddess Nemesis gave him a taste of his own medicine.

Alas for poor Echo, that justice came much too late. When she tried to let Narcissus know how she felt, she could only repeat the last few words of what he said. Her strange behavior caused him to flee. Ultimately she pined away, heartbroken, and turned into a stone, though she retained the power of a disembodied voice.

FAUNUS

Faunus, the son of Jupiter and Calisto, is represented as a horned satyr—half man and half goat—holding to his lips the strange set of pipes invented by the Greek god Pan, with whom Faunus is often identified.

The origin of those pipes is perhaps one of the most popular legends attached to this deity. One day Pan spied a water nymph named Syrinx and approached her with lustful intentions. She fled, and her father, River Ladon, turned her into a reed to camouflage her. Unable to find her among the other reeds, Pan cut several into various shapes and fastened them together, creating what we still call a *syrinx* or a set of *panpipes.*

Faunus's appearance (cloven-hoofed, horn-headed, half goat) and his less-than-proper behavior (namely, his inclination for women and strong drink) have landed him in some undignified settings throughout history. Christianity borrowed Faunus's image for some representations of Satan or Lucifer—the Devil. His Greek counterpart's name, Pan, has been used to describe the sense of fear that sometimes overcomes people—*panic.*

In the Roman pantheon, however, Faunus was not necessarily evil. Rather, he was the leader of all rural deities. Worshiped by shepherds and farmers, he took the forests, hills, and green meadows as his domain. Today, a derivative of his name, the word *fauna,* is used to mean the group of animals that reside in a particular environment.

On February 15 the Romans held a festival called Lupercalia, in honor of Faunus. It involved young men running through the streets with whips and lashing young women. This was thought to ward off infertility.

FLORA

lora was the Roman goddess of spring flowers, gardens, and perpetual youth. She was the wife of the west wind, Zephyrus. Often she is represented as carrying flowers and wearing a crown flowers.

Her reputation, unfortunately, seems to have been besmirched by some of her followers. The festivals dedicated to this "goddess of all that flourishes" took on a rather racy tone. Called floralia, the festivals are said to have featured bawdy, farcical, sometimes indecent stage productions, with courtesans and prostitutes taking part. As a result, the name Flora has supposedly been popular among women of "ill repute" at various times in history.

For example, a prostitute named Flora is noted as a favorite lover of Pompey the Great in early Rome, and some writers say she attained the status of a deity by donating to the city the fortunes she earned through her illicit activities. Most historians, however, dismiss that theory as anti-pagan propaganda produced by early Christian writers. In fact, the goddess Flora was worshiped by ancient peoples long before the founding of Rome. Thus, even if there was a Roman prostitute named Flora, it was not she who became the goddess.

The Greeks knew Flora as Chloris. Today Flora's name is closely associated with her dominion, flowers, and when we want to refer to the entire collection of plants in a certain region, we call it the area's *flora*.

JUNO

uno, the daughter of Saturn and Ops, was one of the children that Saturn swallowed at birth. Rescued by her brother Jupiter, she later married him, and they had several children together, including Mars, the god of war, and Vulcan, the god of destructive fire.

Many of the myths surrounding Juno stem from her jealousy of Jupiter's other relationships. Juno spent a great deal of time wreaking vengeance on Jupiter's lovers as well as on the illegitimate children who had been fathered by Jupiter.

Of all the great god's illegitimate offspring, none boiled Juno's blood more than Hercules, who was a source of great pride to Jupiter. Even before Hercules was born, the intrigue began. Juno tricked Jupiter into promising that the next royal male born would be named high king. Then she slowed the labor of Hercules' mother and accelerated another woman's childbirth. This infuriated her adulterous husband.

As fate would have it, though, Juno herself was tricked into suckling an orphaned baby, who turned out to be Hercules. By nursing him, she made the object of her hatred immortal. Legend says that when she discovered who it was at her breast, she pulled the child away, and the resultant spray formed the heavenly band of light that we know as the Milky Way.

Matronalia, a special festival celebrated by the Romans on March 1, was held in Juno's honor. She presided over marriages, aided women in childbirth, and was a special counselor and protector of the Roman state. June, the sixth month of the year, is named for her.

JUPITER

he grandest and most powerful of the Roman gods, Jupiter was far from the benevolent ruler that we might like to imagine. Jupiter's legend is fraught with immoral behavior and merciless punishments.

The youngest son of Saturn, Jupiter was the only off-spring of that tyrant not devoured at birth. His mother, Ops, saved him from being eaten. When he grew up, Ops secretly established him as Saturn's cup-bearer, and he used that position to advantage. Jupiter laced his father's drink with an emetic that made Saturn vomit, expelling Jupiter's previously devoured siblings. Jupiter then led the group in a successful rebellion against Saturn.

Unlike the gods of many later religions, Jupiter is not credited with creating humans or their universe. In the wake of numerous chaotic events, he did establish some sense of order among the gods. Order in his own behavior, though, was another story. His wife, Juno, became so angered by her husband's numerous affairs that she led a revolt against him, which landed her in chains until she promised never again to oppose him.

Historically, Jupiter came to Roman mythology by assimilation of the Greek god Zeus. By the time Rome became an imperial force, Jupiter in some form was viewed as the supreme god of the 47 Latin confederation cities.

Also known as Jove, Jupiter is often represented as a majestic, bearded figure seated on a golden or ivory throne, holding lightning in his right hand and a scepter in his left hand. Near him often an eagle soars.

MARS

Called Ares by the Greeks, Mars was chiefly known as the Roman god of war. He was highly valued by a particular sector of Roman society—the Roman Legions. According to his legend, that appreciation was reciprocated. He liked the soldiers as much as they admired him.

Mars was said to have been fond of the sounds of conflict—the clash of steel on steel, the shouts of victory and screams of defeat. He often took whatever measures necessary to incite men to fight. Unlike his Greek counterpart, who was given little credit for strategic prowess, Mars was regarded an invincible hero. Oddly, though, he was also considered the god of seers and shepherds, and he presided over spring, the start of the agricultural year.

Mars was a son of Jupiter and Juno. The ancient poets indicate that Juno produced him by touching a flower—an effort to rival the miraculous feat of Jupiter in producing Minerva from his head. Mars might also be called the grandfather of Rome, because two of his children—the twins Romulus and Remus—are credited in legend with establishing the ancient city.

The month of March, the first on the Roman calendar, was named after Mars. Today his name is linked to all things military through our word *martial*. We also apply his name to the "red planet," the fourth from the sun in our solar system.

MERCURY

ercury was the son of Jupiter and Maia, a daughter of Atlas. He was the god of commerce and wealth, in addition to music and science. Though he had a long list of other godly duties—such helping mortals achieve eloquence in speech—Mercury's main role was as the messenger or herald of the gods. And he was a swift one at that, touted as moving "fast as the speed of thought" to do Jupiter's bidding.

In a less admirable role, Mercury was also known as a thief. Among other objects, he stole Neptune's trident; the sword of Mars, the war god; the girdle of Venus, the goddess of beauty; and the hammers of Vulcan, the god of blacksmiths and destructive fire. Many of his thefts may merely have been quests for adventure, spurred by his boredom at being an immortal.

He started his life of crime at a young age. The day he was born, he took some cattle that belonged to his older brother Apollo. But he earned little more than a stern rebuke from Jupiter, and he returned to his brother's good graces by presenting Apollo with a lyre he had made from a tortoise shell. This act showed Jupiter that the child had a natural flair for politics, and hence that he was a perfect choice for a personal envoy.

Known as Hermes to the Greeks, Mercury is usually depicted as a young, lively man with wings on his cap and feet. He carries a caduceus, a winged staff with serpents curled around it, now used as a symbol of the medical profession. The planet closest to the sun in our solar system bears his name.

MINERVA

s a deity, Minerva had numerous duties. She served not only as the goddess of wisdom but also as the goddess of arts, science, and war.

According to one of the legends of her origin, she sprang from the head of Jupiter fully grown and adorned in battle armor, bearing weapons. Small wonder that Jupiter had been suffering from a splitting headache! He had brought on this state of affairs by swallowing Minerva's mother, Metis.

In spite of her military appearance at birth, Minerva was credited with inventing the flute, the trumpet, and the earthen pot, as well as numerous agricultural tools, such as the rake, yoke, and plow. Transportation technologies attributed to Minerva included the chariot and the horse bridle. Meanwhile, others knew her as more of a domestic goddess—a patroness of cooking, spinning, weaving, and other so-called womanly arts.

Minerva was a vain but modest goddess. She took no lovers, and when a man once happened to witness her bathing, she permanently blinded him.

The goddess is said to have been introduced to Rome between 715 and 675 B.C. Many of her traits were assimilated from the Greek goddess Athene. Together with Jupiter and Juno, Minerva formed the high triad of chief deities in the Roman pantheon.

According to the renowned mythologist Thomas Bulfinch, Minerva's favorite bird was the owl, which remains a symbol of wisdom to this day. She also had a penchant for olives, which she considered sacred.

MOMUS

omus, a son of the goddess Nox, was the Roman god of laughter. But his was typically not the fun, healthy, good-natured kind of laughter. Instead, he was given to mockery and censure.

To understand the barbed nature of his humor, it helps to know his background. His mother, Nox (Nyx to the Greeks), was Night personified, and she is said to have sprung directly from Chaos to deliver dark forces upon the earth. In addition to Momus (Mockery), her offspring included Death (Thanatos), Misery, Sleep (Somnus), Vengeance (Nemesis), and the Fates.

In such company, a little mockery doesn't seem all that bad. Nonetheless, Momus made a nuisance of himself by continually satirizing the gods. When Vulcan created a man out of clay, Momus pointed out the folly of not putting a window in the man's breast so that his true thoughts and feelings could be seen. Likewise, he viciously teased Minerva for not making her house moveable so that it could be placed wherever the situation was most favorable. While such wit may not sound particularly funny or cruel by today's standards, in the Romans' society—and aimed at their gods—it may have seemed quite sharp.

Similar themes may be seen in medieval systems. In the Middle Ages some nobles employed court jesters to keep the spirits of the court high. This called for some teasing and ribbing now and then. Still, like Momus, the jesters could get in trouble if they were too sarcastic. Today people sometimes use the term *momus* to refer to an individual who is constantly finding fault.

NEPTUNE

eptune was a son of Saturn and Ops. His siblings included Jupiter, Juno, and Pluto. When it came time to divide the kingdom of his father, whom he helped overthrow, the seas became Neptune's domain.

Worshiped under many names, Neptune ruled the waves and was the god of ships and all maritime affairs. Originally a god of springs and streams, he later became identified with the Greek god Poseidon. Neptune was second in power only to Jupiter, and he ruled from a great palace beneath the sea.

His wife, Amphitrite, was one of the Nereids, a race of beautiful sea nymphs. Neptune and Amphitrite had two sons: Triton, the trumpeter of the seas, and Proteus, who could see the future and change his appearance at will. Neptune also had a daughter, Thetis, who is said to have been the mother of the Greek hero Achilles.

As god of the seas, Neptune is blamed for summoning furious ocean storms and for raising sea monsters to attack the heroes of numerous legends. In other stories, however, he is credited with subduing storms. He could do any of these things, at his pleasure.

Legend also has it that he produced the first horse to be seen and used by mortals. Smiting the earth with his trident, he created a chasm from which the animal leaped forth. In appreciation, Neptune was named the patron of horse racing.

Neptune is commonly represented as standing in a giant seashell drawn over the waves by horses. In his hand he holds the trident, symbol of his power over sea, rivers, and fountains. The Romans celebrated his festival on July 23.

OPS

he Romans regarded Ops as the mother of their current race of gods. Ops was the daughter of Coeus (Uranus) and Gaia (Mother Earth). To the Greeks she was commonly known as Rhea.

Ops came to Italy when she married Saturn, who was also a child of Coeus. Saturn by then had toppled Coeus and taken his throne. After Ops had borne several children to Saturn, she began to realize that he was extremely fearful because of a dark prophecy that one of his own offspring would overthrow him—as he had done to Coeus. This paranoia led her husband to the peculiar habit of swallowing his newborn children.

When it came time to deliver her youngest child, Jupiter, Ops's maternal instincts took over. She craftily wrapped a stone in swaddling blankets and left it for the nervous Saturn to devour. Secretly she turned the real child over to his grandmother, Gaia, to be raised in safety. When Jupiter matured, he returned to his father's house and forced Saturn to regurgitate the other children, who then joined Jupiter in bringing on Saturn's downfall and ultimate demise.

Though this new order of gods initially honored Ops for her role in their survival and triumph, Jupiter later became angry when she warned him about the dangers of his lust. She then faded into relative obscurity, though she did appear in minor roles in the tales of lesser gods.

In one of those legends, Ops is said to have been the first deity who fortified the walls of cities with towers. Hence she is often depicted wearing a crown of towers.

ORPHEUS

O rpheus was a son of the muse Calliope. His paternity, however, is in dispute. Some sources say that his father was a mortal, others that it was the god Apollo.

Orpheus himself was a mortal, a famous poet and musician. Given a lyre (a kind of harp) by Apollo, he became wonderfully accomplished with the instrument. On earth he had no rival in his musical ability. His playing could enchant rocks, trees, and wild beasts. Rivers would change their direction to follow his lovely sounds. However, his joyous song turned tragic on his wedding day.

As Orpheus's bride, Eurydice, was fleeing from the pursuit of a former lover, she was stung in the foot by a serpent. She died, and the musician, driven by misery, descended to the Underworld to retrieve her. Impressed by this mortal's resolve, Pluto decided to allow her to follow Orpheus back to the upper world, on one condition—that Orpheus not turn around to look at her until they reached the surface. Of course, he did look, and Eurydice was recalled to her fate.

Overcome by grief, Orpheus then wandered the hills until a fierce band of Thracian women slew him and threw his head into the river Hebrus. According to legend, the river began to murmur from its murky depths, "Eurydice . . . Eurydice." Finally his head was carried to the island of Lesbos, where some sympathetic muses buried it.

Orpheus's famous lyre, according to the myth, was placed in the night sky as the constellation Lyra.

PLUTO

When Saturn's children overthrew him and divided up his kingdom, the heavens went to Jupiter, the seas to Neptune, and the nether regions, or Underworld, to Pluto.

Also known by the names Hades, Dis, and Orcus, Pluto was the third son of Saturn and Ops. Swallowed by his father at birth, Pluto was later freed by Jupiter and joined his siblings in vanquishing their father. During this epic struggle, Pluto used his helmet of darkness, which gave him the ability to see in the night.

As lord of the infernal regions, he was charged with overseeing the spirits of the dead. There he became romantically frustrated, having no female companion with whom to share his dark kingdom. It seems that the goddesses were eager to be wooed by the ruler of the Underworld. All of his invitations went unanswered.

Undaunted, Pluto became even more determined to find a goddess to wed at any cost. Eventually he fell in love with Proserpine (or Persephone), the daughter of Ceres. One day, when he spied her gathering flowers, he opened the earth with a stroke of his mighty two-pronged fork and abducted the goddess, carrying her screaming to his subterranean kingdom. When her absence was discovered and reported to Jupiter, a deal was struck in which Proserpine agreed to remain with Pluto in the Underworld for three months out of the year. These three months became the season we know as winter.

PLUTUS

Plutus, the god of riches and wealth, may have been the ancients' attempt to give a godly face to the unpredictable cycles of nature's bounty.

Plutus was the son of Ceres, the goddess of agriculture. Initially he was the god of the bountiful harvest, personifying one aspect of his mother's dominion. However, as the civilizations that worshiped him evolved into more commercial societies, Plutus became more closely associated with the financial prosperity a good harvest could bring its producer.

He was said to be a fickle, arbitrary divinity—qualities shared by nature itself. In some years, good weather and other factors produce an abundance of crops, while in other years harvests are poor. Ancient societies, dependent on the land and always afraid of famine, were especially sensitive to these cycles of good and bad seasons, which they could neither predict nor control. They tended to attribute the fluctuations to the character of the god who was responsible, rather than simply to the prevailing weather patterns and ground conditions.

Plutus is often represented as blind because—again, like nature itself—he bestowed his gifts indiscriminately, not caring who deserved them and who did not. Because his rewards could come slowly and gradually, he is sometimes shown as lame. But also, because his blessings could rapidly fly away, he is given wings in some representations.

POMONA

omona was the goddess of fruit orchards. A minor divinity, she had a temple in her honor at Rome, where the priests would offer her sacrifices for the preservation of their fruit.

Pomona was the only wood nymph who did not cherish the wild forests. Instead, she delighted greatly in the cultivation of fruit-bearing gardens and orchards. Pomona was a lovely maiden, but she was so caught up in her work that she often received her admirers coldly. She had little time or inclination for romance.

There was one suitor, though, who managed to get her attention. This was Vertumnus, who fell so deeply in love with her that he resorted to visiting her gardens in various disguises just to be able to look at her.

Finally, when seeing her was no longer enough, he came to her disguised as an old crone and told her how beautiful she was. Then he kissed her. This startled the goddess, but she listened intently as Vertumnus compared her to a vine without a tree.

He then revealed his true appearance to her. He told her that he shared her love of the orchards and would be content to spend his life working by her side. He also reminded her about Venus's wrath against hard-hearted women who spurned lovers. Pomona ultimately yielded to his combination of beauty, eloquence, and determination, and she accepted Vertumnus as her lover.

Illustrations of Pomona generally show her with a basket full of fruit or flowers.

SATURN

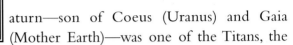

Saturn—son of Coeus (Uranus) and Gaia (Mother Earth)—was one of the Titans, the race of Elder Gods who possessed incredible size and strength. Ruler of the known universe, Saturn was married to Ops, who later was patterned after the Greek goddess Rhea. Their children included Jupiter, Juno, Pluto, Neptune, and Ceres.

Fearful of a prophecy that one of his children would overthrow him, steal his kingdoms, and take his life, Saturn began to devour his offspring at birth. However, Ops tricked him by wrapping a stone in blankets in place of their youngest son, Jupiter, whom she spirited him away to be raised in secret by Gaia. When Jupiter grew up, he returned as Saturn's cup-bearer, and he gave his father a drink that made him regurgitate the devoured children, who then joined Jupiter in the foretold rebellion.

After being overthrown by his children, Saturn supposedly fled to Italy, where he ruled during the Golden Age. This was said to have been a time of perfect peace and happiness. Saturnalia, a seven-day festival in honor of the god and his Golden Age, was held each year beginning on December 17.

In Roman mythology Saturn began as the ancient god of agriculture. He was originally known as the protector of the sowers of seed, and his wife, Ops, aided the harvesters. Saturn was later assimilated into the likeness of Cronus from Greek mythology. Even so, some of his earlier traits persisted, and he was often represented as a bearded man bearing a sickle and an ear of corn.

SOMNUS

Somnus was the Roman god of sleep. According-ing to legend, his home had no gates because their hinges might creak and wake the inhabitants.

A son of Erebus and Nox (otherwise known as Nyx, or Night), he was one of the infernal deities. Even more infernal, perhaps, was his twin brother, Death. Somnus presided over the realm of sleep. One of his sons, Morpheus—a god of dreams and a shape-shifter—stood watch over him to prevent any loud noises from waking him.

This slumberous family dwelt in a dark cave located far to the west of the world where the sun never shone. Silence reigned supreme. The rooster's morning call was strictly forbidden. In fact, no animals were allowed to make their distinctive sounds, and even tree branches were banned from rustling in the wind.

Near this dreary domicile flowed Lethe, the River of Forgetfulness. Poppies—beautiful flowers with narcotic and hypnotic powers—grew in abundance there, as did many other sleep-inducing plants. Somnus's mother, Night, collected the juices of these plants and scattered them over the earth.

Known as Hypnos to the Greeks, Somnus is often represented as a young person reclined in a profound slumber, holding poppies in his hand and using another bunch of the flowers as a pillow. Though he is described as "a dull god," his power to induce sleep is said to have been effective on gods and mortals alike.

VENUS

enus was the goddess of desire and of the graces. She was generally recognized as the daughter of the sky and the sea. Actually, the legend of her origin contends that she arose fully grown from the foam of the crashing surf after Saturn threw Coeus into the sea.

Venus's role as a deity was to make love and inspire romantic passion in others. She is said to have been so beautiful that grass and flowers sprang forth from the spots where her bare feet touched the earth. Some legends say that she was clothed by the seasons, which perhaps meant that she typically wore little else.

Because her ravishing beauty left nearly all the gods desiring her, she could have had her choice of husbands. But Jupiter, who had adopted her as a daughter, made her marry the deformed but artistic blacksmith Vulcan.

Though she was wed to the blacksmith, the war god, Mars, fathered some of her children. This betrayal became a great weight on Vulcan's heart, and he decided to set a trap for the two adulterers. When they were caught, Vulcan summoned all the gods to pass judgment on his wife and her lover. At the trial, most of the male gods, especially the fleet-footed Mercury, were distracted by Venus's beauty, and they spoke up on her behalf. Ultimately the gods refused to punish Venus or Mars.

In Greek mythology Venus was known as Aphrodite.

VESTA

esta was the Roman goddess of the hearth and fire. Her fire differed greatly from that represented by the blacksmith Vulcan. His fire could be a destructive force, but Vesta's was emblematic of pure, life-sustaining heat.

Vesta was a daughter of Saturn and Ops, and a sister to Jupiter, Neptune, Pluto, and Juno. In addition to the hearth and fire, she also represented the notion of personal security and the sacred duty of hospitality.

Vesta is said to have been mild-mannered, charitable, and proper. She declined to participate in the wars of gods or mortals, always spurned the advances of men, and helped to preserve peace in the home of the gods.

At her altar in Rome there was an order of celebrated priestesses known as the Vestals, or Vestal Virgins. Their chief employment was to prepare the sacrifices and to keep the shrine's sacred fire constantly burning. These priestesses typically came from Rome's most prominent families, and they wielded a significant amount of power. They were required to keep themselves pure for 30 years: 10 years of learning, 10 years of performing, and 10 years of teaching.

While the goddess herself is reputed to have been kind and long-suffering, her followers were not as softhearted. If a Vestal Virgin broke her vows, a funeral service was held for the girl and she was buried alive.

CHRONOLOGY

753 B.C.	Founding of the city of Rome.
560 B.C.	Temple of Diana founded.
509 B.C.	Temple of Jupiter founded.
497 B.C.	Temple of Saturn founded.
493 B.C.	Temple of Ceres founded.
431 B.C.	Temple of Apollo founded.
390 B.C.	Invading Gauls from northern Italy sack Rome.
264 B.C.	Start of First Punic War; Romans defeat Carthaginians in 241.
218 B.C.	Start of Second Punic War; Hannibal crosses Alps into Italy.
202 B.C.	Hannibal defeated at Zana; Carthage sues for peace and leaves Spain.
149 B.C.	Start of Third Punic War; Romans take Carthage in 146.
49 B.C.	Julius Caesar invades Italy.
44 B.C.	Julius Caesar is murdered.
A.D. 43	Roman invasion of Britain by Claudius.
A.D. 64	Great fire sweeps through Rome.
A.D. 79	Mt. Vesuvius erupts.

A.D. 166   Plague sweeps Roman Empire.

A.D. 247   Goths cross Danube River to begin raids on
Roman Empire.

A.D. 250   Roman provinces raided by wandering Franks.

A.D. 395   Visigoths renounce allegiance to Rome and
invade Greece and Italy.

A.D. 409   Vandals fight Romans while invading Gaul
(France) and Spain.

A.D. 410   Rome sacked by Visigoths led by King Alaric.

A.D. 455   Rome sacked by Vandals and other "barbarian"
tribes.

A.D. 476   Last of the Roman western emperors deposed.

A.D. 486   Frankish leader Clovis I overthrows last Roman
emperor in Gaul.

A.D. 493   Theodoric becomes first Gothic ruler of western
Roman Empire.

A.D. 533   Vandals vanquished by General Belisarius under
Byzantine Emperor Justinian.

A.D. 568   Italy invaded by the Lombards.

INDEX ∞

Further Reading

Adkins, Leslie and Roy. *Introduction to the Romans: The History, Culture and Art of the Roman Empire.* London: Quintet Publishing, 1991.

Bierlein, J. F. *Parallel Myths.* New York: Ballentine Books, 1994.

Bulfinch, Thomas. *Bulfinch's Mythology.* New York: Avenel Books, 1979.

Comte, Fenand. *The Wordsworth Dictionary of Mythology.* Ware, England: Wordsworth Editions, 1994.

Flaum, Eric. *The Encyclopedia of Mythology: Gods, Heroes and Legends of the Greeks and Romans.* New York: Michael Friedman Publishing Group, 1993.

Macrone, Michael. *By Jove! Brush Up Your Mythology.* London: Pavillion Books, 1993.

Perowne, Stewart. *Roman Mythology.* London: Hamlyn Publishing Group, 1969.